Printed in Great Britain
by Amazon

44447884R00069